A Primary Source Guide to

PORTUGAL

Elizabeth Rose

The Rosen Publishing Group's

PowerKids Press™
PRIMARY SOURCE

New York

For Emma Bean Destito, for whom the world has just begun

Published in 2004 by The Rosen Publishing Group, Inc.
29 East 21st Street, New York, NY 10010

First Edition

Editor: Natashya Wilson
Book Design: Haley Wilson
Book Layout: Kim Sonsky
Photo Researcher: Adriana Skura

Photo Credits: Cover © Tony Aruza/CORBIS; p. 4 © Geo Atlas; pp. 4 (inset), 20 (inset) © Peter Bennet/The Viesti Collection, Inc.; pp. 6, 16 (inset), 20 © Walter Bibikow/The Viesti Collection, Inc.; p. 8 © Charles O'Rear/CORBIS; p. 8 (inset) ©Vanni Archive/CORBIS; p. 10 The Granger Collection; pp. 12, 14 ©Hulton/Archive/Getty Images; p. 16, 18 © The Viesti Collection, Inc.; p. 16 (inset) ©Hans Georg Roth/CORBIS.

Rose, Elizabeth.
A Primary Source Guide to Portugal / Elizabeth Rose.
     v. cm.— (Countries of the World : A Primary Source Journey)
Includes bibliographical references and index.
Contents: Where is Portugal?—Living with the sea—Romans, Visigoths, and Moors—The Age of Discovery—Portugal's colonies—Changes in government—Portugal's economy—Saints' days and pilgrimages—Portugal today—Portugal at a glance.
  ISBN 0-8239-6733-6 (library binding)
1. Portugal—Juvenile literature. [1. Portugal.] I. Title. II. Series.
  DP517 .R68 2004
  946.9—dc21
                                                          2002015653

Manufactured in the United States of America

Contents

ATLANTIC
OCEAN

Douro River

Porto

Coimbra   Serra
            da Estrela

Fátima

Lisbon   Tagus River

Sesimbra   Évora

PORTUGAL

Madrid

SPAIN

Strait of Gibraltar

Azores Islands

Ponta Delgada   São Miguel

Portugal

Madeira Islands

MOROCCO

Where Is Portugal?

Portugal is a country that is about the size of the state of Indiana. It is located in southwestern Europe. Portugal shares the Iberian **Peninsula** with Spain. Spain makes up about 80 percent of the peninsula. The remaining 20 percent is the country of Portugal. Portugal is 362 miles (583 km) long, and about 150 miles (241 km) wide at its widest point. About 10 million people live in Portugal. This number includes the people of the Azores and Madeira, islands that belong to Portugal. The Azores consists of nine islands that lie 900 miles (1,448 km) west of Portugal. Madeira is one large island and several tiny ones just off the west coast of Morocco.

◀ Spain is the only country that borders Portugal. Portugal's western border is the coast of the Atlantic Ocean. *Inset*: Belém Tower, built 1515–1521, guards the mouth of the Tagus River near Lisbon.

SESIMBRA

Living with the Sea

Five hundred miles (805 km) of Portugal borders the Atlantic Ocean. The ocean controls the weather in Portugal and has given the country its fishing **tradition**. Northern Portugal is cooler and rainier than the south. Portugal gets about 40 inches (102 cm) of rain per year. The **temperature** is about 50°F (10°C) in winter and about 70°F (21°C) in summer. Portugal's biggest rivers are the Tagus and the Douro. They flow from Spain through Portugal to the sea. Many of Portugal's mountain **ranges** also begin in Spain and end in Portugal. The highest mountain range in Portugal is in the center of the country. This range, the Serra da Estrela, is 6,532 feet (1,991 m) tall at its highest peak.

◀ These colorful fishing boats are docked in the harbor at Sesimbra, a coastal fishing town on the Setúbal Peninsula in southwest Portugal. *Inset:* The island of Madeira is known for having weather that is neither too hot nor too cold.

Romans, Visigoths, and Moors

People have lived on the Iberian Peninsula for at least 45,000 years. During this time, many different peoples have claimed Portugal. Around 201 B.C., the Romans took the peninsula from the Celtic tribes that lived there. The Romans called the peninsula Lusitania, for the name of a Celtic tribe. In the fifth century A.D., **barbarians** known as Visigoths attacked Lusitania. The Moors from North Africa took over in 711. In the eleventh century, Spain drove the Moors out of the area and renamed it Portocale. This name was later changed to Portugal. In 1143, Spain recognized Portugal as an **independent** kingdom. Portugal then entered into a golden age of exploration and wealth.

◀ The Moors brought the idea of decorating with tiles to Portugal. Today Portugal is famous for its tiles. This Moorish archway is in Sintra.
Inset: Romans built this temple in Évora in the second or third century A.D.

The Age of Exploration

The sixteenth century in Europe is known as the Age of Exploration. During this century, many explorers set out from Europe to see the rest of the world. The Age of Exploration in Portugal began in the fifteenth century, when Prince Henry of Portugal opened a school for sea captains and **navigators**. Because of the work of Henry the Navigator, as the prince was known, Portuguese sailors and navigators became the best in the world. In 1497, Portuguese explorer Vasco da Gama became the first European to sail to India. Thanks to da Gama, Portugal was able to trade with Africa and India. They were the first Europeans to reach Indonesia, China, Japan, and Australia.

◀ Henry the Navigator is pictured in this 1453 book entitled *Chronicle of the Discovery and Conquest of Guinea*, by Gomes Eanes de Zurara.
Inset: This detail from Abraham Oertel's 1590 map of the Pacific Ocean shows the *Victoria*, famous Portuguese explorer Ferdinand Magellan's ship.

Portugal's Colonies

Portugal's explorations brought much wealth to the country. They also led Portugal to start colonies. By the mid-1500s, Portugal had colonies in Africa, Brazil, India, Malaysia, Indonesia, and China. Portugal got spices from Asia, gold from Africa, and diamonds from Brazil. Portugal kept its colonies for about 400 years. However, Portugal had too many colonies to run them all smoothly. In 1822, Brazil became independent. Indian troops took back Portugal's Indian colonies in 1961. By 1976, Portugal had lost most of its colonies. In 1999, Portugal returned the colony of Macao to China. Today only the former colonies of Madeira and the Azores are still part of Portugal.

◀ Portugal fought to keep its African colonies for more than 13 years. The African wars hurt Portugal's economy, and people were angry. In April 1974, military officers overthrew Portugal's government and ended the fighting in Africa. These Portuguese soldiers and tanks were part of the takeover.

Changes in Government

In 1910, **revolutionaries** overthrew Portugal's king, Manuel II, and declared Portugal a **republic**. However, the new government had troubles. From 1910 to 1926, the government leadership changed 40 times! In 1926, the army overthrew the government. A man named Antonio de Oliveira Salazar ran Portugal from 1932 until 1968. He turned the government into a **dictatorship**. In 1974, a **revolt** resulted in Portugal becoming a republic once again. Today the people of Portugal elect the president and a **parliament**. The president chooses a **prime minister** to help run Portugal.

◀ This picture of Antonio de Oliveira Salazar was taken around 1950. Salazar did a lot to help Portugal, which was very poor when he became dictator. He was also very strict about running the country his way. People remember him as both a smart leader and a leader who used threats to stay in power.

Portugal's Economy

As Portugal lost its colonies, its economy became very weak. Joining the **European Union** in 1986 has helped Portugal to

build its economy. Portugal is one of the world's largest producers of olive oil and cork. Farmers also grow almonds, figs, and other fruits. Port is a wine that is made in Portugal from grapes grown in the Douro valley. Fishers fish for sardines, lobster, codfish, and tuna. Portugal also produces clothing, glass, pottery, and wood. Portugal is world famous for its lace, pottery, and tiles. About 21 million visitors travel to Portugal and its markets each year.

◀ Cork comes from the bark of cork oak trees, which grow well in Portugal's climate. Portuguese cork is used to make about 80 percent of the world's bottle stoppers. By Portuguese law, bark can only be taken off a cork oak tree once every nine years. *Inset*: This pottery is for sale at a market in Estremoz. *Above*: The euro became Portugal's official money on January 1, 2002.

BAPTISMO DE CRISTO

Saints' Days and Pilgrimages

About 90 percent of the people in Portugal are Roman Catholic. Most others are Protestant, Jewish, or Muslim. Each city and village in Portugal has its own Catholic saint, who is known as the **patron saint** of that city. For example, Saint Vincent is the patron saint of the city of Lisbon. On most weekends in Portugal, some village or city is celebrating its saint's day. These celebrations, or *festas*, as they are called, often include a parade, feasting, singing, and dancing as well as a visit to church. Many people also travel to certain holy places or churches to honor a particular saint. This kind of trip is called a **pilgrimage**.

◄ A crowd celebrates Saint John's Day in Vila do Conde. *Inset:* On May 13 and October 13 each year, thousands of people make a pilgrimage to Fátima, the center of faith in Portugal. On May 13, 1917, three children said that a shining figure of the Virgin Mary spoke to them at Fátima.

Portugal Today

Today Portugal has much to offer its people and visitors. It is the base of the Portuguese-speaking world, which numbers about 200 million people worldwide. The Portuguese are proud of their language, which came from the Latin spoken by the ancient Romans. Portuguese people love soccer and bullfights. Unlike bulls at a Spanish bullfight, bulls are not killed during Portuguese bullfights. The Portuguese also adore children and welcome them everywhere. Most of Portugal's people live in coastal fishing villages, but the populations of the largest cities, Porto and Lisbon, grow each year. Portugal remains a country with an exciting past and a bright future.

◀ Traffic flows through the Marques de Pombal roundabout in the city of Lisbon. *Inset:* In Portugal, bullfighters, called *cavaleiros*, fight on horseback. Once the cavaleiro has speared the bull, other men called *forcados* wrestle the bull. Bulls are not killed during fights, but most die soon afterward.

Portugal at a Glance

Population: 10,328,000

Capital City: Lisbon, population 556,797

Largest City: Lisbon

Official Name: Portuguese Republic

National Anthem: "A Portugesa"

Land Area: 35,672 square miles (92,390 sq km)

Government: Republic

Unit of Money: Euro

Flag: Portugal's flag is red and green and shows a seal. The green stands for hope, and the red for the blood shed to create the first republic of Portugal. The seal includes a navigator's instrument and a white-and-red shield decorated with seven yellow castles and five blue shields. Each blue shield has five white dots on it.

Glossary

barbarians (bar-BER-ee-unz) People who are thought to be mean or wild.

dictatorship (dik-TAY-ter-ship) A government run by one person.

European Union (yur-uh-PEE-in YOON-yun) A group of countries in Europe that work together to be friendly and to better their economies.

independent (in-dih-PEN-dent) Free from the control of others.

navigators (NA-vuh-gay-terz) People who steer ships.

parliament (PAR-lih-mint) The lawmakers of a country.

patron saint (PAY-trun SAYNT) A special saint who is thought to help an individual, a trade, a place, a group, or an activity.

peninsula (peh-NIN-suh-luh) An area of land surrounded by water on three sides.

pilgrimage (PIL-gruh-mij) A journey to a sacred or godly place.

prime minister (PRYM MIH-nih-ster) The leader of a government.

ranges (RAYNJ-ez) Rows of mountains.

republic (ree-PUB-lik) A form of government in which the authority belongs to the people.

revolt (rih-VOHLT) To fight or rebel.

revolutionaries (reh-vuh-LOO-shuh-ner-eez) People who fight to change a government.

temperature (TEM-pruh-cher) How hot or cold something is.

tradition (truh-DIH-shun) A way of doing something that has been passed down over time.

Index

Primary Source List

Cover. Castle and fortress overlooking Marvao, Portugal. Christians won this site from the Moors in 1166. The current castle was built in 1299 by King Dinis. It is located about 5 miles (8 km) from the Spanish border.

Page 4. Belém Tower. Commissioned by Manuel I and built 1515–1521, the tower is one of Portugal's best-known landmarks.

Page 8. Archway in Sintra, Portugal, designed and tiled in the Moorish style. Photographed by Charles O'Rear, July 26, 1996.

Page 8 (inset). Roman temple in Évora, Portugal, dating from the second or third century A.D. Photographed by Ruggero Vanni.

Page 10. Portrait of Prince Henry the Navigator, plus text, from *Chronicle of the Discovery and Conquest of Guinea*, 1453.

Page 10 (inset). Detail from Abraham Oertel's map of the Pacific Ocean, 1590.

Page 12. Photograph of soldiers and tanks on the streets of Portugal during the revolution of April 1974.

Page 14. Photograph of Antonio de Oliveira Salazar, Portuguese dictator, ca. 1950.

Page 16 (inset). Photograph of a pottery stall at a market in Estremoz, Portugal. Photographed by Hans Georg Roth, ca. 1985–95.

Page 17. Five-euro banknote. One euro is equal to 100 cents in the euro currency.

Page 18. Saint John's Day celebration in Vila do Conde, Portugal.

Page 18 (inset). Worshipers at the shrine in Fátima, Portugal, photographed by Walter Bibikow.

Page 19. Bullfight in Lagos, Portugal, photographed by Peter Bennett, 1991.

Web Sites

Due to the changing nature of Internet links, PowerKids Press has developed an online list of Web sites related to the subjects of this book. This site is updated regularly. Please use this link to access the list:
www.powerkidslinks.com/pswc/pspo/